45

AFRICAN WRITERS SERIES

*Editorial adviser · Chinua Achebe*

46

Letters to Martha

# AFRICAN WRITERS SERIES

# LETTERS TO MARTHA

and other poems
from a South African Prison

---

## DENNIS BRUTUS

**HEINEMANN**

LONDON · NAIROBI · IBADAN

Heinemann Educational Books Ltd
48 Charles St., London W1X 8AH
POB 25080 Nairobi · PMB 5205 Ibadan

EDINBURGH   MELBOURNE   TORONTO
SINGAPORE   HONG KONG   AUCKLAND

ISBN 0 435 90046 3
© Dennis Brutus 1968
First published 1968
Reprinted 1969, 1970

Printed in Malta
by St Paul's Press Ltd

# Contents

# *Longing*

Can the heart compute desire's trajectory
Or logic obfusc with semantic ambiguities
This simple ache's expletive detonation?

This is the wordless ultimate ballistic
Impacting past Reason's, Science's logistics
To blast the heart's defensive mechanism.

O my heart, my lost hope love, my dear
Absence and hunger mushroom my hemispheres;
No therapy, analyses deter my person's fission:

My heart knows now such devastation;
Yearning, unworded, explodes articulation:
Sound-swift, in silence, fall the rains of poison.

*August 1960*

# *Letters to Martha*
# 1

After the sentence
mingled feelings:
sick relief,
the load of the approaching days
apprehension —
the hints of brutality
have a depth of personal meaning;

exultation —
the sense of challenge,
of confrontation,
vague heroism
mixed with self-pity
and tempered by the knowledge of those
who endure much more
and endure . . .

*Letters to Martha*

# 2

One learns quite soon
that nails and screws
and other sizeable bits of metal
must be handed in;

and seeing them shaped and sharpened
one is chilled, appalled
to see how vicious it can be
— this simple, useful bit of steel:

and when these knives suddenly flash
— produced perhaps from some disciplined anus —
one grasps at once the steel-bright horror
in the morning air
and how soft and vulnerable is naked flesh.

# 3

Suddenly one is tangled
in a mesh of possibilities:
notions cobweb around your head,
tendrils sprout from your guts in a hundred
        directions:

why did this man stab this man for that man?
what was the nature of the emotion
and how did it grow?
was this the reason for a warder's unmotived
        senseless brutality?
by what shrewdness was it instigated?

desire for prestige or lust for power?
Or can it – strange, most strange! – be love,
        strange love?
And from what human hunger was it born?

*Letters to Martha*

# 4

Particularly in a single cell,
but even in the sections
the religious sense asserts itself;

perhaps a childhood habit of nightly prayers
the accessibility of Bibles,
or awareness of the proximity of death:

and, of course, it is a currency —
pietistic expressions can purchase favours
and it is a way of suggesting reformation
(which can procure promotion);

and the resort of the weak
is to invoke divine revenge
against a rampaging injustice;

but in the grey silence of the empty afternoons
it is not uncommon
to find oneself talking to God.

# 5

In the greyness of isolated time
which shafts down into the echoing mind,
wraiths appear, and whispers of horrors
that people the labyrinth of self.

Coprophilism; necrophilism; fellatio;
penis-amputation;
and in this gibbering society
hooting for recognition as one's other selves
suicide, self-damnation, walks
if not a companionable ghost
then a familiar familiar,
a doppelgänger
not to be shaken off.

*Letters to Martha*

# 6

Two men I knew specifically
among many cases:
their reactions were enormously different
but a tense thought lay at the bottom of each
and for both there was danger and fear and pain —
drama.

One simply gave up smoking
knowing he could be bribed
and hedged his mind with romantic fantasies
of beautiful marriageable daughters;

the other sought escape
in fainting fits and asthmas
and finally fled into insanity:

so great the pressures to enforce sodomy.

# 7

Perhaps most terrible are those who beg for it,
who beg for sexual assault.

To what desperate limits are they driven
and what fierce agonies they have endured
that this, which they have resisted,
should seem to them preferable,
even desirable.

It is regarded as the depths
of absolute and ludicrous submission.
And so perhaps it is.

But it has seemed to me
one of the most terrible
most rendingly pathetic
of all a prisoner's predicaments.

# 8

"Blue champagne" they called him
– the most popular "girl" in the place;
so exciting perhaps, or satisfying:
young certainly, with youthful curves
– this was most highly prized.

And so he would sleep with several
each night
and the song once popular on the hit-parade
became his nickname.

By the time I saw him he was older
(George *saw* the evil in his face, he said)
and he had become that most perverse among
the perverted:
a "man" in the homosexual embrace
who once had been the "woman".

# 9

The not-knowing
is perhaps the worst part of the agony
for those outside;

not knowing what cruelties must be endured
what indignities the sensitive spirit must face
what wounds the mind can be made to inflict on itself;

and the hunger to be thought of
to be remembered
and to reach across space
with filaments of tenderness
and consolation.

And knowledge,
even when it is knowledge of ugliness
seems to be preferable,
can be better endured.

And so,
for your consolation
I send these fragments,
random pebbles I pick up
from the landscape of my own experience,
traversing the same arid wastes
in a montage of glimpses
I allow myself
or stumble across.

# 10

It is not all terror
and deprivation,
you know;

one comes to welcome the closer contact
 nd understanding one achieves
w    one's fellow-men,
fellows, compeers;

and the discipline does much to force
a shape and pattern on one's daily life
as well as on the days

and honest toil
offers some redeeming hours
for the wasted years;

so there are times
when the mind is bright and restful
though alive:
rather like the full calm morning sea.

# 11

Events have a fresh dimension
for all things can affect the pace
of political development —

but our concern
is how they hasten or delay
a special freedom —
that of those the prisons hold
and who depend on change
to give them liberty.

And so one comes to a callousness,
a savage ruthlessness —
voices shouting in the heart
"Destroy! Destroy!"
or
"Let them die in thousands!" —

really it is impatience.

11 *November* 1965

# 12

Nothing was sadder
there was no more saddening want
than the deadly lack
of music.

Even in the cosy days
of "awaiting trial" status
it was the deprivation
and the need
that one felt most.

After sentence,
in the rasping convict days
it grew to a hunger
— the bans on singing, whistling
and unappreciative ears
made it worse.

Then those who shared one's loves
and hungers
grew more dear on this account —
Fiks and Jeff and Neville
and the others

Strains of Eine Kleine Nachtmusik
the Royal Fireworks,
the New World,
the Emperor and Eroica,
Jesu, joy of man's desiring.

Surreptitious wisps of melody
down the damp grey concrete corridors

Joy.

[13]

# 13

"At daybreak for the isle,"
and
"Look your last on all all things lovely,"
and
"So, for a beginning, I know
there is no beginning."

So one cushions the mind
with phrases
aphorisms and quotations
to blunt the impact
of this crushing blow.

So one grits to the burden
and resolves to doggedly endure
the outrages of prison.

Nothing of him doth change
but that doth suffer a seachange . . .

*Letters to Martha*

# 14

How fortunate we were
not to have been exposed
to rhetoric

— it would have falsified
a simple experience;
living grimly,
grimly enduring

Oh there was occasional heroic posturing
mainly from the immature
— and a dash of demagogic bloodthirstiness

But generally
we were simply prisoners
of a system we had fought
and still opposed.

# 15

Extrapolation
is the essential secret of our nature
– or so one may call it:

the capacity
to ennoble
or pervert
what is otherwise
simply animal
amoral and instinctual

and it is this that argues for us
a more than animal destiny
and gives us the potential
for the diabolic
or divinity.

# 16

Quite early one reaches a stage
where one resolves to embrace
the status of prisoner
with all it entails,
savouring to the full its bitterness
and seeking to escape nothing:

"Mister,
this is prison;
just get used to the idea"

"You're a convict now."

Later one changes,
tries the dodges,
seeks the easy outs.

But the acceptance
once made
deep down
remains.

*Letters to Martha*

# 17

In prison
the clouds assume importance
and the birds

With a small space of sky
cut off by walls
of bleak hostility
and pressed upon by hostile authority
the mind turns upwards
when it can –

– there can be no hope
of seeing the stars:
the arcs and fluorescents
have blotted them out –

the complex aeronautics
of the birds
and their exuberant acrobatics
become matters for intrigued speculation
and wonderment

clichés about the freedom of the birds
and their absolute freedom from care
become meaningful

and the graceful unimpeded motion of the clouds
– a kind of music, poetry, dance –
sends delicate rhythms tremoring through the flesh
and fantasies course easily through the mind:
– where are they going
where will they dissolve
will they be seen by those at home
and whom will they delight?

[18]

# 18

I remember rising one night
after midnight
and moving
through an impulse of loneliness
to try and find the stars.

And through the haze
the battens of fluorescents made
I saw pinpricks of white
I thought were stars.

Greatly daring
I thrust my arm through the bars
and easing the switch in the corridor
plunged my cell in darkness

I scampered to the window
and saw the splashes of light
where the stars flowered.

But through my delight
thudded the anxious boots
and a warning barked
from the machine-gun post
on the catwalk.

And it is the brusque inquiry
and threat
that I remember of that night
rather than the stars.

20 *December* 1965

[19]

# *Postscripts*
# 1

These are not images to cheer you
— except that you may see in these small acts
some evidence of my thought and caring:
but still I do not fear their power to wound
knowing your grief, your loss and anxious care,
rather I send you bits to fill
the mosaic of your calm and patient knowledge
— picking the jagged bits embedded in my mind —
partly to wrench some ease for my own mind.
And partly that some world sometime may know.

# 2

There are of course tho' we don't see them
— I cut away the public trappings to assert
certain private essentialities —
some heroic aspects of this all
— people outside admire, others pity —
but it is not of these I wish to speak;

but to pin down the raw experience
tease the nerve of feeling and expose
it in the general tissue we dissect;
and then, below this, with attentive ear
to hear the faint heartthrob —
a flicker, pulse, mere vital hint
which speaks of the stubborn will
the grim assertion of some sense of worth
in the teeth of the wind
on a stony beach, or among rocks
where the brute hammers fall unceasingly
on the mind.

# 3

The seagulls, feathery delicate
and full of grace when flying
might have done much to redeem things;

but their raucous greed and bickering
over a superflux of offal –
a predatory stupidity

dug in the heart with iron-hard beak
some lesson of the nature of nature:
man's ineradicable cruelty?

# 4

The wind bloweth where it listeth
and no man knoweth whence it came

And we poor temporary mortals
probationary in this vale of tears
damned and blissful in due course
must wait some arbitrary will
to determine our eternal destiny.

# 5

There were times in my concrete cube
– faceless both the nights and days –
when the arbitrary wind gusted
and I, desolate, realised
on how other things I hung
and how easily I might be damned.

# 6

A studious highschoolboy he looked
— as in fact I later found he was —
bespectacled, with soft-curved face
and withdrawn protected air:
and I marvelled, envied him
so untouched he seemed to be
in that hammering brutal atmosphere.

But his safety had a different base
and his safely private world was fantasy;
from the battering importunities
of fists and genitals of sodomites
he fled: in a maniac world he was safe.

# A Letter to Basil

How deadly an enemy is fear!
How it seeks out the areas of our vulnerability
and savages us
until we are so rent and battered
and desperate
that we resort to what revolts us
and wallow in the foulest treachery.

To understand the unmanning powers of fear
and its corrosive action
makes it easier to forgive.

And there is even room for pity.
For how will you endure
the occasional accusatory voice
in your interior ear,
and how will you, being decent, not sorrow?

11 *November* 1965

Presumably
one should pity the frightened ones
the old fighters
who now shrink from contact:
and it is true I feel a measure of sadness
– and no contempt –
and have no wish to condemn
or even grow impatient

But it is best to shutter the mind and heart
eyes, mouth and spirit;
say nothing, feel nothing and do not let them know
        that they have cause for shame

# *For Bernice*

You were the still oasis
in a whirling vortex
(though it would surprise you)
and I rested with such content
in the thought of you
and our relationship:
true, it was not perfection,
but there seemed to be a shared richness
and you could make such chords of sensibility
sing in me
and permit them resonance
in the chamber of your listening self
that thinking of you
I was simply glad.

11 *November* 1965

# Blood River Day

*[For Daphne Edmondson]*

Each year on this day
they drum the earth with their boots
and growl incantations
to evoke the smell of blood
for which they hungrily sniff the air:

guilt
drives them to the lair
of primitiveness
and ferocity:

but in the dusk
it is the all pervasive smell of dust
the good smell of the earth
as the rain sifts down on the hot sand
that comes to me

the good smell of the dust
that is the same
everywhere around the earth.

16 *December* 1965

The impregnation of our air
with militarism
is not a thing to be defined
or catalogued;
it is a miasma
wide as the air itself
ubiquitous as a million trifling things,
our very climate;
we become a bellicose people
living in a land at war
a country besieged;
the children play with guns
and the schoolboys dream of killings
and our dreams are full of the birdflight of jets
and our men
are bloated with bloody thoughts; inflated sacrifices
and grim despairing dyings.

# *Their Behaviour*

Their guilt
is not so very different from ours:
— who has not joyed in the arbitrary exercise of power
or grasped for himself what might have been another's
and who has not used superior force in the moment
     when he could,
(and who of us has not been tempted to these things?) —
so, in their guilt,
the bared ferocity of teeth,
chest-thumping challenge and defiance,
the deafening clamour of their prayers
to a deity made in the image of their prejudice
which drowns the voice of conscience,
is mirrored our predicament
but on a social, massive, organised scale
which magnifies enormously
as the private deshabille of love
becomes obscene in orgies.

*Blood River Day 1965*

[28]

*For X.B.*

It is a way of establishing one is real;
personal, intimate and civilised:
to shout, be violent or importune
will not do in this context,
but a confrontation, male-female,
is possible, even if not legitimate or moral:
so one hopes, strives, speculates:
it is the wish to be accepted as a person
— something real and living.

*For Daantjie—on a* New Coin *envelope*

On a Saturday afternoon in summer
greyly through net curtains I see
planes on planes in blocks of concrete masonry
where the biscuit factory blanks out the sky

Cézanne clawing agonisedly at the physical world
wrested from such super-imposed masses
a new and plangent vocabulary
evoking tensions, spatial forms and pressures
almost tactile on the eyeballs,
palpable on the fingertips,
and from these screaming tensions wrenched
new harmonies, the apple's equipoise
the immobility of deadlocked conflicts
− the cramp, paralyses − more rich
than any rest, repose.

And I, who cannot stir beyond these walls,
who shrink the temptation of any open door
find hope in thinking that repose
can be wrung from these iron-hard rigidities.

[*While under house arrest*]

[30]

*For E.C.*

Equipoise
Like this is rare,
And thus your gifts are doubly dear:
Intellect moves strong and clear
Nobly matched by nature –
Enchanting fusion, grave and fair!

One wishes for death
with a kind of defiant defeatism

wishing that the worst may befall
since the nearly-worst has so often befallen:

it is not a wish for oblivion
but a pugnacious assertion of discontent

a disgust at the boundless opprobrium of life
a desperation; despair.

2 *July* 1966

# *Prayer*

O let me soar on steadfast wing
that those who know me for a pitiable thing
may see me inerasably clear:

grant that their faith that I might hood
some potent thrust to freedom, humanhood
under drab fluff may still be justified.

Protect me from the slightest deviant swoop
to pretty bush or hedgerow lest I droop
ruffled or trifled, snared or power misspent.

Uphold – frustrate me if need be
so that I mould my energy
for that one swift inenarrable soar

hurling myself swordbeaked to lunge
for lodgement in my life's sun-targe –
a land and people just and free.

    3 *July* 1966

*For Canon L. John Collins*

Now that we conquer and dominate time
hurtling imperious from the sun's laggard slouch
transcendentally watching the Irish jigsaw
slip astream dumbly under masking cloud,
green England dissolved in history-grey
and fanatic old Yeats made mellow by height,

now that all canons of space-time are dumb
and obey the assertions of resolute will
and an intricate wisdom is machined to leash
ten thousand horses in world-girdling flight,
how shall we question that further power
waits for a leap across gulfs of storm;

that pain will be quiet, the prisoned free,
and wisdom sculpt justice from the world's
　　　　　jagged mass.

> 5 *August* 1966 [11.38]
> *En route from London to New York*
> *El Al Airlines*

Above us, only sky
below, cloud
and below that
cloud;
below that
sea;
land is abolished,
only the sky and air and light
a beatific approximation
achieved.

After this power
this conquest of brute reality
what can we not not do
not abolish?

Peace will come.
We have the power
the hope
the resolution.
Men will go home.

> 5 *August* 1966
> *In flight over the Atlantic*
> *after leaving South Africa*

# The Mob

[*The white crowd who attacked those who
protested on the Johannesburg City Hall steps
against the Sabotage Bill.*]

These are the faceless horrors
that people my nightmares
from whom I turn to wakefulness
for comforting

yet here I find confronting me
the fear-blanked facelessness
and saurian-lidded stares
of my irrational terrors
from whom in dreams I run.

O my people

O my people
what have you done
and where shall I find comforting
to smooth awake your mask of fear
restore your face, your faith, feeling, tears.

*May* 1962

# *Train Journey*

Along the miles of steel
that span my land
threadbare children stand
knees ostrich-bulbous on their reedy legs,
their empty hungry hands
lifted as if in prayer.

*July* 1962

# On The Island
## 1

Cement-grey floors and walls
cement-grey days
cement-grey time
and a grey susurration
as of seas breaking
winds blowing
and rains drizzling

A barred existence
so that one did not need to look
at doors or windows
to know that they were sundered by bars
and one locked in a grey gelid stream
of unmoving time.

## 2

When the rain came
it came in a quick moving squall
moving across the island
murmuring from afar
then drumming on the roof
then marching fading away.

And sometimes one mistook
the weary tramp of feet
as the men came shuffling from the quarry
white-dust-filmed and shambling
for the rain
that came and drummed and marched away.

# 3

It was not quite envy
nor impatience
nor irritation
but a mixture of feelings
one felt
for the aloof deep-green dreaming firs
that poised in the island air
withdrawn, composed and still.

# 4

On Saturday afternoons we were embalmed in time
like specimen moths pressed under glass;
we were immobile in the sunlit afternoon
waiting;
Visiting time:
until suddenly like a book snapped shut
all possibilities vanished as zero hour passed
and we knew another week would have to pass.

# On The Road

The moon is up; the trees detach
themselves from formless landscapes
to assume a courtly grace,
cloud-bank scatters are light-edged blades
that pale the sparse occasional stars.

The wide night sighs its sensuous
openness, stirring my mind's delight
to a transfiguring tenderness
as stars harden to spearpoint brilliance
and focus fierce demands for peace.

*January* 1963

# On The Beach

Seablue sky and steelblue sea
surge in cubist turbulence,
dissolve, reform in fluid light
and cadences of sandsharp breeze;

spindrift from sand-dunes tresses down
to inlets where rock-fragments shoal,
seaspray and statice distil the mood
salt-sweet, foamwhite, seaweed-brown.

All in this jagged afternoon
where rock, light, sand and sea-air sing,
brown hair and air-live skin complete
this transitory plenitude.

The companionship of bluegum trees
their sheen and spangle against the midday winter sun
and the companionable nudge of my heart
knocking against my mind and memory
with evocation of my student hazy days
condemns me once again
labels me poet dreamer troubadour
unreal unworldly muddle-headed fool
while the trees nod and swagger
and the level sunlight flows.

8 *July* 1966

Steeling oneself to face the day
girding one's self for the wrap of clothes
bracing oneself for the thrust of the world
one buckles to buttons and zips and belts:
With the gritted reluctance and indifference to pain
with which one enters an unsought fight
one accepts the challenge the bullying day thrusts down.

# *Nightsong: Country*

All of this undulant earth
heaves up to me;
soft curves in the dark distend
voluptuous-submissively;
primal and rank
the pungent exudation
of fecund growth ascends
sibilant clamorously:
voice of the night-land
rising, shimmering,
mixing most intimately
with my own murmuring —
we merge, embrace and cling:
who now gives shelter, who begs sheltering?

*April* 1962

Abolish laughter first, I say:
Or find its gusts reverberate
with shattering force through halls of glass
that artifice and lies have made.

O, it is mute now – not by choice
and drowned by multi-choired thunder –
train wails, babies' sirens' wails:
jackboots batter the sagging gate
the wolfwind barks where the tinplate gapes,
earth snarls apocalyptic anger.

Yet where they laugh thus, hoarse and deep
dulled by the wad of bronchial phlegm
and ragged pleuras hiss and rasp
the breath incites a smouldering flame;
here where they laugh (for once) erect –
no jim-crowing cackle for a watching lord,
no sycophant smile while heart contracts –
here laugh moulds heart as flame builds sword.

Put out this flame, this heart, this laugh?
Never! The self at its secret hearth
nurses its smoulder, saves its heat
while oppression's power is charred to dust.

*Mid-fifties*

After the entertainment
the couples go to bed
their sense sharp to just the pitch
for erotic excitement,
husband and wife
with tastes aroused by shared delight
lover and beloved merged in the glow of sensation
lesbian, jaded boss and para with their various thrills
licit or illicit with a special added touch;
after the entertainment
Beethoven with his sonorous percussive exultation
veldfiring to the scored climactic roar
or the stripteaser with a special grossness
thrusting obscenities to the furtherest act
her shouting viewers urged her to;
after the current ballet, premiered show
the bawdy singer in the cabaret
the coupling couples turn to bed.

11 *July* 1966

No, I do not brim with sorrow;
Anger does not effervesce
In viscerally rancid belches
Or burst its bubbles on my optic nerves;
Gall is not secret in my parotids
Nor hatred fetid on my breath:

Only the louse of loneliness
Siphons the interstitial marrows
Of my brain: the inaccessible itch
Mesmerises hands, heart and flesh
Devouring all my scabrous desolate tomorrows.

1960

Cold

the clammy cement
sucks our naked feet

a rheumy yellow bulb
lights a damp grey wall

the stubbled grass
wet with three o'clock dew
is black with glittery edges;

we sit on the concrete,
stuff with our fingers
the sugarless pap
into our mouths

then labour erect;

form lines;

steel ourselves into fortitude
or accept an image of ourselves
numb with resigned acceptance;

the grizzled senior warder comments:
"Things like these
I have no time for;

they are worse than rats;

[48]

you can only shoot them."

Overhead
the large frosty glitter of the stars
the Southern Cross flowering low;

the chains on our ankles
and wrists
that pair us together
jangle

glitter.

We begin to move
       awkwardly.

*Colesberg*

Let me say it

for no-one else may
or can
or will
or dare

I have lashed them
the marks of my scars
lie deep in their psyche
and unforgettable
inescapable.

Of course there were others who served
and much that I could not have done
but I am a part of the work
and they connect it with me

they know I have done them harm

they who are artists in deprivation
who design vast statutory volumes
and spend their nights in scheming deprival

I have deprived them

that which they hold most dear
a prestige which they purchased with sweat
and for which they yearn unassuagedly
— their sporting prowess and esteem
this I have attacked and
blasted
unforgettably.

The diurnal reminders excoriate their souls

Amid a million successes
— the most valued on fronts where they were under attack —
they grimace under the bitter taste of defeat

their great New Zealand rivals
the Olympic panoply and Wembley roar
for them these things are dead
are inaccessible
unattainable

nowhere else does apartheid exact so bitter a price
nowhere else does the world so demonstrate its disgust
in nothing else are the deprivers so deprived.

And they know I will do more.

What wonder such gingerly menacing claws,
they would rend me if they could
(and perhaps will)
but I accept their leashed-in power
and the cloaked malice of their gaze
and wait
anger and resolution

yeast in me
waiting for the time of achievement
which will come if God wills
when I flog fresh lashes across these thieves.

2 *July* 1966

# I

Our aims our dreams our destinations

Thought reconstructed in vacuity

A dialogue:
But God doesn't answer back.

Say then we fear
we hope
we speculate
prognosticate,
what intractable arguments
coil round us
wrestle us Laocoön-like,
and what unnameable horrors
ultimate despair
shudder
and owl-moan hollowly
at the unseen ends
of the dark corridors of the brain.

There looms the threat —
a tight knot forming in the viscera —
of defiant rebellion
so of self-elected damnation —
the only kind a benignant God
makes feasible
— so one feels it
in the tenuous proliferate tendrils of thought.

Well if He damn me,
drive me to damnation
by inflicting the unendurable,
force me along the knife-blades till I choose
perdition
how shall I feel guilty?
When my sense of justice says
*He* drove me
He damned me
He's the guilty one
and if He chose —
BE DAMNED TO HIM


And then to spend eternity
eternally in revolt
against injustice-justice
fighting in vain
against injustice
in the service of my private justice
against a God turned devil
hoping forever for the triumph of despair.
"Evil be thou my Good."

# II

The inherent impulse to good
an inbuilt aspiration
integrated
impossible of disentanglement;
what does it argue?


Is it the seed
from which man grows to divinity
— and, before it,
can God stand condemned?


Before what superior standards
is God found inadequate
His mercy finite and inferior to our own?


And where does compassion
degenerate into sentimentality?


(Pity me! Pity me God! I cry
And imply, not mercy
but a fellow-feeling;
and so?
Impute to him equality
or denigrate his super-humanity
and make it inferior to our own?)

(But he was human once —
or so we are assured
and so can find no human state
beyond the range of his experience
or knowledge:
— but always other depths remain
obscurities of knowledge
divine protectedness,
insulations from our woe)

So we must grapple.

And agony
engenders desperation;

then agnosticism;

then, perhaps
an agonised truth
(truthfulness)

Is He the Infinite Hangman?
Executioner?
Torturer?

Must we be driven to the edge,
racked on the precipice of the world?

For what dread guilt
are these dread exactions made,
the extortion of blood and sighs?

Can we find hope
in thinking that our pain
refines us of our evil dross,
prepares us for a splendid destiny?

or in a fellow-link
a shared enterprise
the splendid Gethsemane
which must purchase redemption for the world
and by our agony
pay debts to buy
the pardon for the world

suffering humanity!
transfigured humanity!
Ecce homo!

*1 March 1966*